On

Nights

I

Hurt

Also by Deonte' Earl Towner

(Poetry)

Pieces in the Dark: Turn the Light On

Secretly Unhappy: Please Don't Tell

Fading into the Clouds

On

Nights

I

Hurt

Deonte' Earl Towner

Printed in the United States of America

First Printing, 2023

Instagram: @deontetowner
@deontetownerpoetry
Website: www.deontetowner.com
Cover Design: Alejandro Baigorri
ISBN: 979-8-218-17356-2

To those who are tired of fighting themselves…

War Over My Soul

Dear God,

I have given you countless reasons to let me go, but you still love me.

You could have passed me over, but your voice inside of my head kept pulling me back to your love. I still don't understand why you did not give up on me. I still don't understand why you still want to use me. I am no good.

Don't you see all of the things that I have done?

Don't you hear my secret thoughts?

Don't you see what I do when no one is looking?

Thank you for looking beyond my faults and chasing after my soul.

Amen

Leave It in the Past

Your past mistakes and failures do not define who you are. We have all done things that we are too ashamed to talk about.

You don't have to live in the past anymore. God wants you to stop beating yourself up over who you used to be. You aren't doing God a favor by being angry at yourself. You have a new life and a future with God on your side.

Leave it in the past.

You have been forgiven.

Another Chance

Dear God,

Thank you for giving me another chance. I don't deserve the love that you continually show me each and every day.

You took me out of situations that I caused myself. You stopped me from hurting myself when I didn't want to be alive anymore.

You pulled me out of danger when I was around the wrong crowd.

Many people did not make it out alive, but you gave me another chance.

Amen

A Change of Seasons

Stop distancing yourself from God when times get hard.

Stop questioning him.

He's pulled you out of situations before, and he will do it again.

You have already won the victory before the battle even started.

Breathe!

Old Battle Wounds

Dear God,

I used to be angry because I did not understand why you kept allowing certain things to happen in my life. I questioned you when I should have trusted the process, but now I am mature enough to understand that I had to go through all of those battles to get to where I am today.

I do not regret the pain that I had to endure from the past anymore. Each day I choose to look forward and not look back. Each day I choose to be grateful and not bitter. Thank you for giving me the strength to never give up.

You have brought me from a mighty long way.

Amen

No More Hiding

Compa, you okay?

I'm good.

I'm fine.

I'm chillin...

But God knows deep down inside that you are sad, angry and haven't been feeling yourself lately.

Give it to God and let him work out the things you're hiding from everyone.

Ignoring the Red Flags

Dear God,

You have shown me the red flags in people, but I ignored you. I try my hardest to see the good in everyone, but I still manage to get hurt.

Please forgive me for ignoring you. I could have avoided certain situations if I would have listened to you from the beginning.

You pulled me out before it was too late. Thank you for rescuing me.

Amen

Replaying in My Head

You will never amount to anything.

You will always be stuck in the same situations.

Those feelings will never go away.

You will always struggle in sin.

You will never find love.

You will be single and lonely forever.

Every relationship you get into will never work.

Only God's power will get rid of the hurtful voices inside of your head that repeatedly tell you that you are not good enough. Don't listen to them. Keep praying until they go away. Those are lies from the enemy.

God's word is the truth.

Lukewarm

Dear God,

I haven't been myself lately. I don't pray like I used to. I have done things that I am not proud of.

I do my own thing even though I know better. I am tired of living lukewarm.

Please forgive me and help me get my life together.

Amen

Old Memories Again

Whenever you feel sad at night and you start thinking about your past a little too much remember you have God.

Don't let those thoughts win.

Fill your mind with God's word. Get on your knees and pray. Prayer is powerful.

You may not feel him all the time but he's there comforting you and working it out.

Made Up Mind

Dear God,

Please give me the strength to stop running back to my old ways. I need to stop giving into sin. You have made me into a new person, but I keep rejecting the new life that you have created for me.

Today I choose you, and I don't want to go back. You are more than enough. I am sorry for putting everything else before you. I hope it's not too late to get it right.

Amen

Another Sleepless Night

God is bigger than anything that is stressing you out. He's already worked it out.

Stressing won't make it better.

Go to sleep.

Struggling to Forgive Myself

Dear God,

You have forgiven me, but I find it challenging to forgive myself. The hurtful memories keep replaying in my head over and over again.

I can't sleep at night. I wake up feeling emotionally drained. I can't shake these feelings. Sometimes I make myself feel guilty because I don't deserve your goodness in my life.

Please God help me let go of the past, so I can finally experience freedom on the inside and live the life that you have created for me.

Amen

Starting Over

When are you going to realize that you don't need their approval? You are losing yourself each time you choose to be someone other than who God created you to be.

Years later you will regret turning into someone you're not. You will look back and think about how far you could have been if you would have stayed with God. Train your mind not to look back on how life could have been and just start over with God. God is waiting for you.

There's nothing wrong with starting over. I know you are filled with regret, but go with God he will take care of the rest.

Uncomfortable Nights

Dear God,

No matter how uncomfortable, sad, hopeless, unstable and rocky my life gets I will always trust you. Nothing could ever pull me away from you.

Whenever I feel low the enemy whispers in my ear about how you aren't there anymore, but you promised that you will never leave me nor forsake me.

During my lonely nights I call upon your name and you comfort me. In times of chaos you said peace be still. You have always kept your promises.

I am forever grateful.

Amen

Undivided Attention

Sometimes your biggest blessings don't come until you allow God to remove certain people out of your life. I know you are worried because they have been in your life for a long time but God is moving you into a new season.

You won't be able to carry every relationship into this new stage of your life. Remember God sees the future. He knows what certain people are capable of doing, and he is trying to protect you. God doesn't want to hurt you.

God needs your undivided attention. He is getting ready to answer your prayers and more, but those things won't come to pass until you obey God's voice and stop trying to do it on your own.

Far Too Long

Dear God,

I secretly struggle with depression and anxiety. Please bring peace and clarity into my life. I have been feeling this way far too long.

Please show me a new way of thinking. I want to experience a new life so I can finally be free. I feel caged inside.

Please deliver me so that I can have everlasting joy that you have promised your people. I give you all of me today. You are invited in.

Amen

Nothing to Worry About

Your enemies can't get in the way of what God has for you. No matter how many of them group up against you.

God will block their attacks and bless you in front of everyone that counted you out.

Your enemies will be so confused they will eventually start fighting amongst themselves while you are living the life that God has called you to live.

Wipe those Tears

Dear God,

I thought I would never be happy again, but you came through once again.

My entire life has been filled with pain, but you gave me joy.

Amen

It's Over

God will take away those lonely feelings you are experiencing at night. He will cure your mind from constantly overthinking.

You don't have to keep hurting yourself at night by looking at old messages and photos from the past.

You don't have to feel drained and unhappy anymore.

It's over.

Protect Me

Dear God,

I am tired of letting the wrong people into my life. I have been broken and abused by people that I thought wanted the best for me. I used to trust people and now my guard is up. At this point I don't know who to trust anymore.

Please protect me from people that pretend to be there for me. Make me aware of those that are trying to get close to me for all the wrong reasons. Guard me from those that are trying to hurt me, and help me open up to those that are genuinely there for me.

Amen

It All Makes Sense

There are nights I randomly get angry because of my past. I think about the people that betrayed me. I think about my old relationships that went wrong, and then I blame myself for not being smarter.

As it gets later at night I begin to realize that God will use all that I have been through to help someone else.

Being used by God doesn't always feel good, but it's worth everything that I had to go through in order help someone else get out of the struggle.

Whatever it Takes

Dear God,

Sometimes it's hard to let go of people that have been in my life for years. I am asking you to free me from any friendships that aren't pleasing to your eyes no matter how much it may hurt.

My relationship with you is far more important than anything else that I am holding onto. I desire to be closer to you. I am willing to do anything it takes to be where you want me to be.

Amen

Stay Focused

Stop trying to control how people see you. Just be who God created you to be.

God wants you to focus on your goals, dreams and the purpose he has given you. The enemy will do anything to distract you. Don't give into the distractions.

Keep praying and reading God's word.

Patiently Waiting

Dear God,

I know you have someone for me. I have been waiting patiently. During this season I have been working on myself. I have been praying more, working on my self-worth, figuring out who you have called me to be and speaking your promises into my life. God give me the courage and the strength to start interacting with people again. I am tired of being alone.

I know the day will come that you bless me with a soulmate, but sometimes I lose hope and begin doubting if love will ever come my way. I have been crushed way too many times.

Maybe I am damaged good. Maybe I can't be loved. But I refuse to believe those lies from the enemy.

I deserve love. I am worthy to be loved. I am not going to be lonely for the rest of my life. You have someone just for me. I thank you for helping me see your plan and purpose over my life.

Father God you are my first love, and I can't wait to see who you have for me.

Amen

One Day

Don't allow the enemy to fool you into believing the world would be a better place without you here.

Rebuke those negative thoughts, and remind yourself that God loves you.

Just know someone is out there praying for your strength.

One day you will wake up and all of these negative feelings will be behind you.

One day this will all be a distant memory. Better days are ahead.

Human

Dear God,

I no longer envy or desire to be like the people I see on social media.

Being who I am is more than enough, and most importantly I just want to be who you created me to be.

Amen

Left on Seen

When your past calls don't answer. God has blessed you with a new life.

Stop looking back and focus on what's ahead of you.

A Different Way

Dear God,

Sometimes I sabotage the good moments in my life because I am used to bad things always happening. I don't allow myself to fully enjoy the moment because I do not want to get hurt again.

I am tired of feeling this way. I don't want to be negative for the rest of my life. Please clear my mind so I can enjoy all the different ways that you are blessing me.

Amen

It's Time to Move On

Some people aren't meant to be in your life forever.

I know you miss the old relationship you had with them. You probably look at old messages they sent you, but God took them out of your life for a reason.

It's time to let them go and free yourself from how things used to be.

On Empty

Dear God,

Show me how good life can be. I am tired of being weighed down with the same problems.

My life has been in complete chaos lately and I do not know what to do anymore. I tried to find peace on my own, but I realized I cannot do anything without you.

Please God forgive me for running away. I surrender my life to you and from this day forward I will follow you completely.

Amen

Nothing Stays the Same

Sometimes in life it may feel as though
everyone is distancing themselves from you.

The conversations aren't the same anymore, and
you are beginning to feel how different things
are becoming.

I know it hurts because of how strong the bond
used to be, but just know God is drawing closer
to you. The relationship you build with him is
far more important than anyone else's.

Afraid of Everything

Dear God,
I struggle with falling asleep at night.

I overthink the conversations I had throughout
the day.
I overthink how people see me on social media.
I overthink how I come off to people.
I overthink about not being good enough.
I overthink about my weight.
I overthink about my future.
I overthink about things I cannot control.
I overthink everything.

Please deliver me from overthinking. I don't
want to feel this way anymore.
Amen

Beating Myself Up

Stop being so hard on yourself. We've all made mistakes and done things we are not proud of. God has forgiven you and he loves you.

He wants you to know that you don't have to carry your past, guilt, shame and burdens into your future.

It's time for you to move on, let go and forgive yourself.

Hidden Sins

Dear God,

I hated the way sin made me feel.

Sin kept me feeling heavy on the inside. I was always trying to hide the things I did from people because I was so ashamed of my life. The enemy told me that life will never get any better, and for a while I believed the lies.

You took me out of the enemy's captivity and promised to give me the strength to never go back.

Amen

Never Ending

When you're mentally going through it God will give you peace of mind.

Distant Memory

Dear God,

When I wake up in the morning I don't think about the pain anymore. I have made peace with my past. The enemy used to harass me, but those tricks don't work on me anymore.

Thank you for helping me take my power back.

Amen

God Knows

There is no pain that God doesn't feel.
There is no struggle that God doesn't
understand. There is no past that God cannot
forgive.

All the Way

Dear God,

Make me whole again. I have fallen back into my old ways. I want to move forward, but I keep forgetting the power that you have given me on the inside. I am tired of living this way.

The empty void inside of me can only be filled with your love.

Forgive me for pushing you away. The further I stray away from you the deeper the hole gets.

I surrender!

This time I want to get it right, and stay with you. No more turning back.

Amen

God Misses You

You cannot hide what you do from God. He knows what you are struggling with. You don't have to live in denial anymore. God requires you to be honest with yourself.

He just wants you to tell him what bothers you.

He wants to be your best friend. You can tell God anything.

What are you waiting for?

He understands that you are not perfect, but he wants you to acknowledge him. He's never left you even when you left him. Let him in. He misses hearing from you.

Please Don't Judge Me

Dear God,

I don't know who to talk to anymore because I don't want people to think there is something wrong with me. I know you are a mind regulator.

You give me strength on days I can't seem to find a reason to smile.

You give me hope on days I feel sad. You give me peace when my life is spinning around. I depend on you for everything because you are my God.

Amen

Just Stop

Stop living inside of your head. God is taking care of everything in your life. Whenever you called on him he answered. Whenever you needed him he showed up.

Why do you keep questioning God?

Why do you keep doubting him when things don't go your way? God has proven to you over and over that he will never fail you.

Breathe and put all your trust in him.

I Give Everything

Dear God,

When will I stop getting hurt by everyone. I give people so much of me, and I never get the same energy back.

Whenever they need me I answer the phone. Whenever they are sad I comfort them. I'm being pulled in all directions. I stress myself out trying to be everything to everyone.

Please send me a friend that will be there for me as much as I am there for everyone else. I deserve to have good people around me too.

Amen

Sooner or Later

God is concerned about you. He wants you to live a fulfilled life. He wants you to have a friend that you can lean on. He wants to bless you with a soulmate that understands who you are. He wants you to accomplish your dreams and aspirations.

He wants you to be full of joy and not sorrow. He wants you to smile and not be sad. God wants the best for you, but you have to trust the process.

Everything happens for a reason. You may not understand it at that moment, but sooner or later it will all make sense.

Facing Reality

Dear God,

I know you hear me.

Please!

I am begging for you to take me out of this situation. I know that I haven't been faithful. I have been hard headed at times. There were times I ignored your voice because I did not want to listen, but Lord I beg you.

Turn this situation in my life around. I promise not to go back to my old ways. I know in the past I have gone back on my word, but this time I mean it. Please hear my cry.

Amen

New Life

Stop being so hard on yourself. Speak positivity into your life. Train your mind to start speaking God's promises. I know you have been through a lot growing up, and you don't have a lot of nice things to say about yourself.

But you are living for God now and he has given you a new life. You have so much to be grateful for. You are not the same person anymore.

Every morning and every night cast the negativity out of your mind until you hear God's voice.

Back to Shore

Dear God,

You saw the skeletons in my closet and cleared them out.

I thought I would have to live in guilt and shame for the rest of my life.

I thought my issues were too big for you to handle.

I thought that you would tell me I am no good.

I thought you could never use no one like me, but then you came into my life like a mighty wind.

You dove into the deepest parts of my heart. You changed my ways, and gave me a fresh new start. Only you…

Amen

What Is It?

What do you need to let go of in order to be at peace and closer to God?

Is it someone from your past you finally need to let go?

Is it an old lover that keeps coming in and out of your life?

Is it a friend that keeps betraying you, but you keep making excuses for them?

Is it a memory that's too painful to let go?

I Will Call

Dear God,

When I can't sleep at night I will call you.

When the world seems so intense and I can't breathe I will call you.

When my heart begins hurting and the memories begin to flood in I will call you.

When I begin tossing and turning at night because my mind starts overthinking again I will call you.

When the wound starts to bleed again I will call you.

When the negative voices start to talk to me at night I will call you.

Amen

Soul Free

Train your mind to stop thinking about the past so much. It is time for you to finally move on and be happy. If you keep allowing your past to keep you sad then you will never be happy.

God wants to bring joy and peace into your life, but you have to surrender it all to him.

You will soon realize his plans are far greater than what you had in the past.

Old things have no room in your future.

No More Running

Dear God,

I am ready to stop running from you. You had plans for my life before I was born. I allowed the enemy to get into my ear, and I decided to go my own way.

My life has been filled with heartbreak and pain. I don't pray like I should because I feel guilty for how many times I ignored your voice. I am afraid to go to church because of all the dysfunction living inside of my head. I am scared because the life that I am living is all I know.

Please give me the courage and strength to submit my life to you. I can't live this way forever. I am running on empty and I want to be full of your spirit. Please save me. I believe your son Jesus Christ died on the cross for my sins. I ask you to forgive me for all that I have done. I am saved in your precious name.

Amen

Acknowledgments: I first give honor to Jesus Christ who is the head of my life. Without him I am nothing. He gets all the credit and glory.

I thank God for my beautiful soon to be wife Yadicza future Mrs. Towner. God truly answered my prayers. You've helped me believe in love again. You are the sun to my life.

I thank God for my wonderful parents Joseph and Emily Towner. My mother is my best friend. She is a prayer warrior and has been there every step of the way for me. My father is still recovering from his stroke please continue to keep him in your prayers.

Also, I thank God for my siblings Natachiana and Joseph Towner. Nina we had some amazing memories we've shared together. I miss our walks around Creekbridge. I miss the times when we would dance in the kitchen. JoJo you are the father I desire to be like when I have kids. You are my Dad and brother.

To my wonderful sister-in-law Amanda. I am so grateful for you. You have a pure soul.

You have brought a beautiful gift in our lives and that is my niece baby Eva.

To my handsome nephew's RJ and Shelton God has so many amazing things in store for you. Just know that Uncle D loves you, and not a day goes by that I don't think about you two.

To my brother-in-law Showbiz thank you for the good times as a kid.

To the rock of my family Big momma you remind me to put everything in God's hands.

Big shout outs to all the Kings on my Instagram. Thank you for sharing your stories with me. We uplift and encourage each other every day. I have never met some of you, but we have created a brotherhood. We will always be compas for life.

To my supporters that I call my friends and family on social media and to my city Salinas the 831, thank you for supporting and always believing in me.

To my Locke students I will never forget you all. Rest in peace to my students Rickey and Daquan. South Central LA misses you.

Romans 10:9